MOORE STREET

GROWING UP IN THE ERA OF JIM CROW

BY DONALD WADDELL LAHUFFMAN

Editor: Vanessa M. Cavett
    Clinton, Mississippi

Cover Designer: HeyDesignGuy LLC
    Baltimore, Maryland

Publisher: G Publishing LLC
    Huntsville, Alabama

ISBN: 979-8-9858131-1-1

Library of Congress Control Number: 2022903459

Published and Printed in the United States of America

Dedication

This book is dedicated to my parents, the late Calvin and Hettie LaHuffman, who provided a wonderful life for me and my siblings.

Acknowledgments

I am grateful to my beloved wife Jean for her love, tolerance, and support in this journey. I would like to thank my oldest daughter, Donna LaHuffman-Coles, and my son, Donald "Joey" LaHuffman, for their moral support and encouragement. My grateful appreciation extends to my youngest daughter, Dr. Renee LaHuffman-Jackson, whose valuable skills assisted me in writing this book. I am thankful to my friends, Karen and Sharon Robinson, from the St. Joseph's Episcopal Church Bible study, for encouraging me more than they realized. Finally, I would like to thank my friend, Samuel Lloyd for all of his assistance with technology to get the documents to my daughter.

Table of Contents

Foreword

This book is written to offer a glimpse into my life growing up in a small town in Southeastern North Carolina during the Jim Crow Era (1942-1960). It centers on Moore Street, which, by all accounts, was in a relatively stable, black working-class neighborhood, located a few blocks from downtown Fayetteville, North Carolina. Moore Street was a part of the "Red Zone Community" in Fayetteville.

I recall life growing up in a neighborhood where Christian values were prioritized. Also, family values were stressed, education was promoted, and a strong work ethic was emphasized. During a time when the forces of segregation and oppression surrounded our communities, Moore Street triumphed, and the children who grew up there were blessed.

Moore Street is a metaphor for all Americans and those coming to America. It symbolizes the human will to succeed despite obstacles and to transcend and triumph over oppression.

Chapter 1: DESCRIPTION OF FAYETTEVILLE, NORTH CAROLINA

Fayetteville, North Carolina is a small city situated along the banks of the Cape Fear River. Located in Southeast North Carolina, it is about an hour's drive from the South Carolina State line. The current population is 200,000. The city was named after Marquis de Lafayette, a French military officer who fought in the American Revolutionary War.

Fayetteville is adjacent to Fort Bragg, North Carolina, one of the world's largest military installations. The city is hot and humid in the summer months with average temperatures ranging from the high eighties to the high nineties on average – very hot! In the winter, average temperatures are in the mid-60s. Despite the weather conditions, Moore Street was an oasis of faith, family, and community to the residents who lived there. It was a haven that protected me from the outside world that was beset with economic disparity and racial unrest. On Moore Street, residents not only survived, but they also thrived.

Moore Street today is a mere shadow of the flourishing black neighborhood it was during the 1940–1960 era. Now Moore Street is filled with vacant lots and centers that provide services for the many homeless who roam the area. Back then, Moore Street was a vibrant neighborhood populated by a prosperous community of upwardly mobile people. Beautiful homes with well-kept yards dotted this affluent street. The residents represented a myriad of professional occupations, including educators, dentists, clergy, businesspeople, and civil service employees.

Historically, the street was home to free blacks after the Civil War, and its location was referred to as "Red Bone" to distinguish it from other neighborhoods in the city. Moore Street is located in an area near downtown Fayetteville and situated between Ramsey Street and Murchison Road. The Moore Street Community consisted of single-family houses, usually one story, situated on well-kept yards. Most of the houses were framed. The house I grew up in was a two-story frame house built by my grandfather, William Waddell. It was later remodeled by my parents, Calvin and Hettie

LaHuffman, who moved there in the early 1940s before my birth.

My parents moved from Philadelphia, Pennsylvania to Fayetteville. My older sister Margaret and my brother Calvin were born in Philadelphia. My younger sister Cynthia and I were born in Fayetteville. Mama said our house on Moore Street was one of the first houses to have indoor plumbing, and people would come by to marvel at our inside bathroom. In that era, people had outhouses instead of inhouse bathrooms.

My parents moved to Fayetteville, so my daddy could develop his business. In Philadelphia, he had invented and marketed a hair product that African American women used to straighten their hair. Then, Dad got a job working on the railway mail. His job involved traveling by train from Fayetteville to Richmond, Virginia to pick up and distribute mail. Later, Daddy was hired as a mail carrier at the Fayetteville Post Office. He was one of the first black mail carriers in Fayetteville. Next, he would be promoted to Finance Superintendent after passing the exams. A decade later, he was promoted to Superintendent of Mails.

Daddy had a sixth-grade education, albeit a brilliant mind. He opened and operated three beauty shops, and at the same time, continued working at the Post Office. Daddy also was a hair stylist during his off-hours. He had customers who would not let anyone else style their hair.

Mama finished Fayetteville State Normal School; however, she did not work outside of the home. Instead, she faithfully and diligently functioned as a wonderful mother and wife who provided a pleasant home for her family. Mama taught us to respect and value people for who they are and how they treat others. Along with our parents, Moore Street was filled with other exemplary adults who also contributed to our lives by their mentorship and positive influence that helped to solidify this great community.

Today, Moore Street may be a place whose luster has dimmed, as it has become known for vacant lots and homelessness. However, from 1942 through the 1960s, it was a place filled with the brightness and vibrancy of proud residents who worked hard to build a successful, cultivated community for their families.

Chapter 2: DOWNTOWN FAYETTEVILLE CIRCA 1940 – 1960

Situated in the center of downtown Fayetteville is the Market House, which by its location, causes traffic to circle it from four directions. Formerly, the Market House was used as a slave market under segregation laws. Needless to say, black Fayetteville citizens have traditionally resented the Market House because it reflects an era of white supremacy and debasement of black people during the Jim Crow Era. Others, notably white people, are equally passionate about maintaining the Market House for sentimental reasons. This controversy continues in our present era.

There was one long street, Hay Street, which was in downtown Fayetteville. Person Street was on the other side of the Market House. The adjacent streets, Green and Gillespie, and smaller streets intersected these main traffic arteries. The main shopping area was located on Hay Street. It was anchored by stores such as Sears Roebuck and Company, Belk-Hendsdale Department Store, Fleishman's Big Store, Miss Vogue, Kress 5 and 10 Cent Store, and Eagles. The Prince Charles Hotel and several movie theaters were also part of this area. The assembly of churches included the Black Presbyterian Church, Haymount Presbyterian, Hay Street Methodist, First Baptist Church downtown, St. John's Episcopal Church on Green Street, St. Joseph's Episcopal Church on Moore Street, Evans Metropolitan AME Zion on Cool Spring Street, and St. Ann's Catholic Church on Cool Spring Street.

A point of interest is that several stores, not all of them, had separate water fountains for whites and colored. As children, we would often drink out of the whites only water fountains. Surprisingly, black people got into trouble for drinking out of the wrong water fountains although it did not seem that the water fountains were actually monitored.

Occasionally, it was big news in the black community when a store hired a colored cashier. This was extremely rare. One grocery store, which our community patronized, hired several black cashiers. However, most black workers were limited to being janitors and maids for white people. A large number of blacks worked at Ft. Bragg as soldiers, government civilians, or laundry workers. Most store clerks, salespersons, and managers in stores where we shopped were white. Government officials and office workers were all white. Usually, when we saw a team of laborers working on city streets, they were black. The white supervisors usually stood back, enjoyed a cigarette, and watched while the black workers toiled. Our strong role models were parents, neighbors, teachers, and ministers. They taught us by precept and example that we did not have to accept limitations in life. We could strive to be anything we wanted to be. I am eternally grateful for the role models that lived in the Moore Street neighborhood.

Chapter 3: ST. JOSEPH'S EPISCOPAL CHURCH

St. Joseph's Episcopal Church stood as a beacon of light on Monroe Street. It truly was the most prominent landmark, located at the corner of Moore and Ramsey Streets, and it played a vital role in my life. The beautiful green church was the gift of benefactor Mrs. Eva Cochran who was a member of St. John's Episcopal Church, the white Episcopal Church on Green Street, a few blocks away.

Mrs. Cochran was a friend of my mother's cousin, Charlotte McNeil, who was her seamstress. Mrs. Cochran wanted her and other blacks to have a nice church to enjoy worship service. After St. John's black worshippers grew tired of having to worship in the balcony, they desired a church of their own; Therefore, they separated from St. John's.

After leaving St. John's, black worshippers founded St. Joseph's Episcopal Church. I could not write about Moore Street without discussing the historic role this vital church had in our community. The church campus consisted of three buildings: the church, the rectory, and the parish house. Both my grandparents and parents attended St. Joseph's Episcopal Church.

This century and a half old church has been a strong refuge for the Black Community throughout the years. The church once served as a service club for black military families when they could not attend the white service club. At one time, the church operated an excellent school. St Joseph's offered some of its lands to the city of Fayetteville to use as a playground; the city used their property for many years for a dollar per year. The Moore Street playground had a baseball field, basketball courts, a tennis court, and a space for table games. A playground supervisor worked during the summer months. Little league baseball and football teams were sponsored by the local Shriners.

Traditionally, St. Joseph's would take the Sunday School children and their parents on a church-sponsored picnic to one of two places. Jones Lake, the state-sponsored recreation spot for blacks, was outside of Elizabethtown, NC. The other site was Atlantic Beach, SC, which was a much longer ride and generally disfavored because of that.

All in all, the picnics were extremely fun for everyone. Our mothers would prepare baskets of goodies for us to eat, and the church would provide hotdogs and soft drinks. Some parents would supply and grill meats for these outings. Mama would usually pack a large lunch: ham and cheese sandwiches, deviled eggs, fried chicken, potato salad, and fruit. Then she placed the food in an ice cooler. As children played in the water, the adults and the lifeguard on duty, always watched them closely. Jones Lake, a state park for colored people, was well maintained and supervised by Mr. Powell, the park superintendent.

Members of St. Joseph's Episcopal Church represented an array of occupations ranging from business owners, educators, civil service workers, physicians, pharmacists, military officers, social workers, FSU faculty and staff, and lawyers. At its peak, membership ranged from 150 to 175. The church always employed a full-time priest who resided on the campus with his family.

Chapter 4: SUMMER MEMORIES

In the 1950s and 1960s, there were only two public swimming pools in Fayetteville. The pool for white people was Lamon Street pool, which was located at the far end of Moore Street, which ran opposite Ramsey Street, the main road leading to downtown. Lamon Street pool was closer to my house than Seabrook pool, which was a few miles away, near the Fayetteville State College Athletic Field. This pool was named Seabrook Pool after Dr. James Ward Seabrook, former president of Fayetteville State Teachers College. Seabrook Pool was the center of a large amount of summertime activity. I could swim all day for 9 cents. Lifeguards were on duty and the pool was well managed. On a somber note, during the polio epidemic, children had to be in the house during the heat of the summer because of public health regulations in the early 1950s.

Although the desire to cool off was a continuing summer quest, nobody I knew had an air- conditioner at home. So, my buddies and I came up with a solution. Downtown Fayetteville had a large department store, Sears, Roebuck and Company, which featured an escalator, and the store was air-conditioned. What fun it was to walk down the railroad tracks to Sears. After walking 15 minutes, we could enjoy total comfort. We would stroll into the store and go up and down the escalators enjoying the coolness, until a store clerk told us to quit. Usually, no one ever stopped us. The clerks treated us kindly. To my friends and me, it was the best treat ever.

Little League Baseball was, undeniably, a highly anticipated summer activity. I was excited to play baseball with the neighborhood team, the Shriners. The age limit to play was 12. We played with real baseballs, and our uniforms resembled the New York Yankees' uniforms.

Before we were old enough to play baseball at the Moore Street Playground, we had fun playing softball on Frink Street. Usually, after a quick early morning breakfast of cereal, we would gather on Frink Street in front of Mr. Jones' Café to begin our softball game. Our game would last until one of our mama's called us home because of the extreme heat. Usually, we would go home a few minutes after we had been called. One friend was hard-headed and would not go home when his mama called. Sadly, years later, his hard-headedness proved fatal. After high school, he was shot in Vietnam because he did not follow orders to not light a cigarette. On Moore Street, we were taught to mind our manners and to respect authority. Although we knew our friend did not always adhere to these teachings, we were grieved to hear of his passing.

After returning home from a game, I would have a peanut butter and jelly sandwich or lunch meat, if we had any. Sometimes my friends came to our house, and we would dine on sandwiches made with ketchup, mayonnaise, or mustard. These were our least favorite.

Wearing our uniforms, we walked to neighboring ball fields to play games. One day while walking to a game across town, the police stopped us and said they received a call that we were making too much noise while walking down Dick Street, which was located in a white neighborhood. This experience was scary for us kids who had no experience with the police. We were terrified. Also, it was disheartening to be judged guilty by accusation without presenting our side of the story. The policemen upheld accusations that were based solely on our skin color.

Even though there were some difficult lessons learned along the way, each day there was a ritual we looked forward to. The ice cream man would come by the neighborhood every afternoon in the summer, and my sister Cynthia and I, along with other neighborhood kids, would worry our parents for a quarter to buy a popsicle. I treasure these times that helped to buffer the harsher moments of life.

In the evening shade, we often gathered on the porch of a neighbor, Mrs. Wilson. She was very good at entertaining us with spooky stories, usually featuring the boogie man or the red-eyed devil. She made up the stories and told them to us with so much expression. Her stories would always frighten us. Around dusk, my sister and I had to go home. We lived right across the hedges from the Wilson house. After hearing her stories, we were glad our house was nearby. Daddy was always at the door waiting for our safe return. Since we did not have a television, we usually came in and went to bed, repeating the routine the next day. We did eventually get a television when I was in the 5th grade.

Chapter 5: BOYHOOD DAYS IN FAYETTEVILLE

Most of the houses in our neighborhood did not have refrigerators, so the iceman delivered ice to customers every other day. Since my buddies and I knew the iceman's schedule, we usually waited in front of my house around 10:00 AM on delivery days. We waited so the ice man could chip off a piece of ice for us from his ice block. He would chip each of us a 3" to 4" piece of ice with his ice pick. Boy! What a nice cold treat. We thought we had something great.

Each house in our neighborhood had a drainage ditch running across the rear backyards. These ditches carried runoff water from the streets back to nearby creeks and ultimately to the Cape Fear River. We liked hanging out around the ditches across our backyards. It felt like we were off on an adventure. Even though we had fun playing in the ditches, we were about to embark on a better play area.

After reaching 10, I was allowed to go up the street to the Moore Street Playground. The playground became our center for summertime activities. At the playground, I could play all types of board games like checkers and Chinese checkers. Many sports were offered like basketball, softball, and volleyball. We could even go to Seabrook swimming pool free each Wednesday if we arrived before 11:00 AM; otherwise, it cost 9 cents. Mama let me go to the pool almost every day that the sun shone brightly. I would stay at the pool most of the morning and leave in the early afternoon. Usually, she gave me a quarter for a pack of crackers and a soda. When my buddies saw me go to the vending machines, they came too, expecting me to share. I always shared, and they did likewise when they had some money. As friends, we looked out for each other.

Across the street from Seabrook pool was the Fayetteville State football field. Outside its fence were a bunch of plum trees. My buddies and I loved looking for plums, blackberries, and grapes. So, we would visit the plum trees after leaving the pool. Usually, the plums were green, and we ended up with stomach aches from eating green plums. However, this did not deter us from eating them.

After being in the pool for hours, my buddies and I would be super hungry. We would head home by walking along the railroad track, which ran behind Fayetteville State College to downtown Fayetteville. From there, we would walk the track to Cumberland Street. Sometimes we would find blackberries in the bushes that surrounded the railroad track. The adults always told us there were snakes in the blackberry bushes, but we never saw any. Perhaps our group was so preoccupied with our revelry that we neither saw them nor heard them rustling in the bushes. Despite many warnings, I did not see a snake until after I became an adult.

On Saturdays and Sundays, our treat was to go to the downtown movie theaters. Our big sister Margaret would take Cynthia and me to either the Colony or Carolina Theatre on Sunday afternoons. These theaters showed movies featuring Spencer Tracy, Elizabeth Taylor, and other big-time movie stars. Daddy and mama had three basic rules for my sister and me: Do not eat at anyone's house and come home when the streetlights come on. Last but not least, if we did not attend Sunday School, we could not go to the movies on Sunday afternoon.

Since I was a member of the School Safety Patrol at North Street School, I could get in the Broadway Theatre for free on Fridays, provided

I arrived there by 4:00 PM. The Broadway showed cowboy movies exclusively, featuring Roy Rodgers, Lash Larue, Whip Wilson, Wild Bill Elliott, Gene Autry, and some of my other favorites.

Chapter 6: A RACIALLY SEGREGATED TOWN

During the years between 1942-1960, Fayetteville was a racially segregated town. Downtown store clerks and municipal employees were all white. Black teachers taught at black schools. Churches were racially segregated. For the most part, black citizens were relegated to lower-paying, non-progressive occupations, such as janitors, maids, yardmen, and kitchen help. Black policemen patrolled black neighborhoods, and they were particularly hard on black soldiers. Local customs authorized black policemen to keep the soldiers in line when they became too unruly in public. Therefore, black officers would execute their authority swiftly and severely. Maybe they wanted to maintain order so the whites would not have to intervene. But we saw it as being overly harsh on their own people.

White privilege was the rule of the day backed by law and tradition. Black people could not eat at white eating establishments. There were separate facilities for whites and colored; water fountains, restrooms, bus station waiting areas, churches, libraries, and schools were all segregated.

I was born two months before the Japanese attacked Pearl Harbor. Post War America was characterized by a high level of prosperity. America became the wealthiest nation. Corporations increased in size, and the automobile industry grew. Meanwhile, here in Fayetteville, racial segregation was strictly enforced. The whites only public swimming pool was off-limits to "colored" who had to use their designated pool even if they resided closer to the white pool. At one time, there was a colored library on Gillespie Street past the bus station; it was the only library blacks were allowed to patronize.

The impact of the terrifying murder of 14-year-old Emmett Till in 1955 in Mississippi awakened me to the extent of the horrors of segregation and racial hatred in America. This brutal murder sent shock waves of indignation and anger throughout America among African Americans. Thanks to black publications like Ebony and Jet magazines, the horror of Emmett Till's lynching was communicated nationwide.

Brown vs. Board of Education of Topeka, Kansas was the transformational Supreme Court decision in 1954. It revoked state laws that established racial segregation in public places. The court ruled that segregated schools were separate and unequal. Unfortunately, the impact of the Brown vs. Board of Education decision was not realized in Fayetteville for years. The city continued to operate a racially segregated school system throughout my time at Fayetteville City Schools. After the court decision, Black students continued to attend all black schools, taught by black teachers in buildings that were substandard. The textbooks used were hand-me-downs from the white schools. This practice was obviously unfair and was intended to keep black students at a disadvantage. However, on Moore Street, our parents and other adults encouraged us to believe things would get better.

Chapter 7: LESSONS FROM HOME: COPING WITH RACISM

My dad was a man of few words, but he insisted that we look people in the eye when talking to them. His advice was especially noteworthy during the era when black men were not expected to look white men in the eye. During this time, it was perceived as disrespectful for a black man to look a white man in the eye. Blacks were expected to be subservient to white people. However, my father taught us that we were not inferior to anyone.

Moreover, my parents taught us the importance of demanding respect as they refused to be called by their first names by white people. After telling me what to say, Mama would send me to a certain downtown department store to pay on her account. When completing the transaction, I was to tell the clerk that the payment was for Mrs. C. W. LaHuffman's account. This was against protocol in the south, as white people customarily referred to all non-white persons by their first names, regardless of their age or status. Hence, it was not uncommon for a young white person to call an elderly black person by his or her first name. Needless to say, Mama did not agree with that protocol.

Mama told us to never take a penny or anything that did not belong to us. She said, "People will test you by leaving coins on tables to see if you will steal." So, always at the forefront of my mind would be the words, do not touch or steal. Lying and stealing were stereotypical behaviors attributed to all black people. Therefore, Mamma always wanted us to be honest.

Moore Street residents believed education was essential to your life. By their words and actions, my parents instilled in each of us the importance of reading and learning. Their plans for us always included college attendance. Even though the opportunities for us to attend college were limited to the segregated college system in North Carolina, we knew we would attend what colleges were available: Fayetteville State, North Carolina College, St. Augustine College, Shaw University, Livingston College, Johnson C. Smith, Elizabeth City College, Kittrell College, Bennett College, Winston-Salem State

Teachers College or A & T College. Mama and Daddy managed to send all four of their children to college with their own financial resources. This was before the era of Pell Grants or other financial aid options for blacks to go to college.

Chapter 8: EDUCATION IN FAYETTEVILLE

My first three years of public school were at Orange Street School located two blocks from our home. Orange Street School was the first modern school for black students in Fayetteville. The school was a two-story brick structure with dimly lit hallways and wooden floors. Teachers at the school were amiable but strict, instructing us in the basics of reading, writing, and arithmetic. There were hardly any disciplinary issues. After receiving a hand spanking or having to write "I will not" a hundred times, students were unlikely to repeat the same offense.

Orange Street School did not have an inside cafeteria. Lunch was served in a facility resembling an elongated storage unit, complete with long handmade tables and benches. A typical lunch consisted of pork liver, rice and gravy, stewed tomatoes, navy beans, hot dogs, vegetable soup, cornbread, gingerbread, and milk. The food was mostly government surplus, yet we had to pay 15 cents for lunch tickets. Recess was held outside on clear days. Boys usually played ball or shot marbles. Girls enjoyed activities like jump rope, hopscotch, or dodgeball. At one time, Orange Street School was the location of E. E. Smith High School.

A more updated modern school was constructed around 1953 on North Street. I attended North Street School from grades 4 through 6. The school was attractive and bright with plenty of windows and an indoor cafeteria and library. In addition, there were clean bathrooms.

Although most of the teachers were female, there were two male teachers, Mr. Burton and Mr. Williams. All the students admired the school custodian, Mr. Joe Quick, who was our mentor and a decent human being. He would warn the boys if we were in trouble with the principal so we could prepare ourselves beforehand. Once, my friends and I left school and headed to the woods behind the campus. Before returning, we wet our hair and faces, so it would appear we had been swimming. Mr. Quick warned us that the principal was looking for us. His warnings always gave us a heads up and made us feel he was looking out for us.

Washington Drive School was the former location of E. E. Smith High School, which was constructed in the mid-1950s. By the time I attended Washington Drive, it was a junior high school that taught grades 7 and 8.

E. E. Smith, the historically black high school in Fayetteville, was a modern, well-run school, headed by longtime principal E. E. Miller. White students attended Fayetteville Senior High School, known today as Terry Sanford High School. Eventually, Fayetteville High's name was changed to Terry Sanford, named after a former Governor of North Carolina. E. E. Smith had strict rules of operation. Students were not to sit on the grass, and students were to walk on the right side of the hallway. Safety patrols and Principal Miller monitored these regulations.

Seating in the auditorium required boys to sit in the side seats as girls sat in the center seats in descending class order. Students were allegedly assigned to homerooms based on academic rank. However, there were other factors more non-academic. Essentially, students from economically advantaged homes were assigned to the higher-class sections. Unfortunately, "the haves and have nots" mentality had seeped into the ranking system of our school.

I served as senior class president and graduated from high school in 1960. Perhaps out of my graduating class of about 160 students, one-third went to college; others entered the workforce or armed services during the fall of 1960. Some colleges my classmates attended were North Carolina A & T State, North Carolina College at Durham, Fayetteville State, Shaw University, Livingston College, Morehouse College, Hampton Institute, Howard University, and Bull City Barber College. For youth who grew up in the Moore Street community, college attendance was expected. The adults' high expectations were the norm for us living in our community. College was the path set forth by our parents, and many of them saw it as nonnegotiable. So, the youth adhered and went to college and began their chosen occupations or careers afterward.

The Moore Street residents were like family. We celebrated accomplishments of individual families and attended funerals of our beloved neighbors. There was a strong comradery amongst the community, and everyone looked out for each other. The legacies of our family bloodlines have flourished through the years and will live for generations to come. Looking back on this heritage, I must recognize the accomplishments of the following amazing men and women from the Moore Street community.

Carolyn Black: Musician/Educator
Arthur Byrd: Educator/Minister
Fred Byrd: Business Executive
Dr. Hurance Cameron: Educator
Anthony Cone: Lieutenant Colonel

Deltricia Currie: Civil Service
Volnetta Clagett: Librarian
Clarence Clagett: Supervisor, Veterans Affairs
Lester Clagett: Social Worker
Harry Carswell: Deputy Sheriff
Dr. James Douglas: Dentist
Sandra Douglas: Educator
Charles Douglas: Corrections Officer
Benjamin Ferguson: Educator/Administrator
Inez Ferguson: Educator
Dr. Nannie Gerald: Educator/Counselor
Olen Gerald III: Industrial Industry
Marvin Gainey: Law Enforcement Officer
Buddy Gainey: Educator
Thelma Gainey: Educator
Marian Gainey: Educator
Margaret Hill: Educator
Frederick Hill: Educator
Bishop Harris: NFL Coach
Arthur Jones: Insurance Agent
Fred Jones: University Finance Executive
Delaney Jones: Counselor
Colon Johnson: Counselor/Retired Army
Allen Kerr: Insurance Agency Owner
Dr. Naomi Kerr: Dentist
Dr. Linda Kerr: University Dean/Minister
Brenda Kerr: Educator
Margaret LaHuffman Wood: Educator
Calvin LaHuffman, Jr.: Educator
Cynthia LaHuffman: Educator

Donald LaHuffman: Educator/Administrator;
School Board Member & Chair
Jimmy Miller: U. S. Navy
Calvin McDonald: Educator
Milton McDonald: School Social Worker
David Morrison: Minister
Doulasina Morrison: Educator
Addie McGuire: Educator
Dr. Lawrence Murphy: Psychiatrist
Deloris Melvin Fowler: Educator
Oliver Melvin: Attorney
Howard Melvin: Computer Industry
Dr. Claude Stephens: Physician
Ralph Stephens: Attorney/Minister
Lynn Vick: Educator/Early
Childhood Administrator
Michael Vick: Attorney
Lawrence Young: Engineer
Mary Lucille Young: Educator

Out of this group of sons and daughters of the Moore Street neighborhood emerged a cadre of educators, a dentist, two physicians, an attorney, ministers, businessmen, college administrators, field grade military officers, computer experts, barbers, and an industrial worker. I salute each of these individuals for making Moore Street proud.

Chapter 9: LEISURE TIME ACTIVITIES

Attending church and Sunday school topped off our weekly activities. There we could see and talk to our peers, find out what was happening in the greater community, and enjoy the general fellowship, which comes from such associations. Nothing was more fun than the Annual Sunday School Picnic held at Jones Lake State Park. The picnic was a family event and was always fun and exciting; it included amazing food, swimming, boating, and laughter. This annual event was a wonderful highlight that we enjoyed so much!

Listening to the radio was a central activity in our family. During that time, stations shut down at midnight. My family would sit in the living room and listen to various programs that were broadcast weekly or sometimes daily over the radio: The Lone Ranger, The Shadow, The

Creaking Door, Super Man, Gabriel Heater, and other popular shows.

The radio was our main entertainment before the invention of the television. We enjoyed listening to the Bill Bowser Show and Jimmy Paye, pioneer Black radio personalities, who played music young people liked, such as rock and roll. They played James Brown, Little Richard, Fats Domino, and many other rock and roll pioneers. I must point out that our dad did not like us to listen to rock and roll music, so we would listen when he was not around.

When television replaced radio, television became a focal point of our family gatherings. Initially, all telecasts were in black and white, yet we were captivated. We enjoyed watching whatever was on. The Ed Sullivan Show on Sunday nights and various variety shows were among our favorites. Every night while watching, we experienced the world outside of Moore Street. And as we watched, we learned.

In the world of sports, our heroes were Joe Lewis, heavyweight boxing champion, and Jackie Robinson, professional baseball pioneer of the popular Brooklyn Dodgers. Musically, my parents favored Louis Armstrong, Pearl Bailey, Nat King Cole, Billy Erskine, and Mahalia Jackson. I idolized these individuals; because of their success in breaking down barriers, they were my role models.

A popular publication in our home was *Ebony* magazine. *Ebony* magazine, in particular, chronicled the lives of black upper-middle and upper-class elite. In addition, we subscribed to *Life* magazine and the local newspaper. These publications provided insight into a world we could not envision within our own community and daily life. We realized the world was much larger than the Moore Street community that we adored.

Before we had a television set, our neighbor, Ms. Jessie Vick would invite us over to watch television. We would enjoy favorites like Howdy Doody, Cisco Kid, and Superman. The Vick's were the talk of the neighborhood because they had the first television. For the first time, we could see images and not have to form our own visualizations of the characters or stories. Today, I realize how gracious Mrs. Vick was for inviting us into her home to watch television. Her generosity and kindness brought us joy. Mrs. Vick was one of the many Moore Street mentors whom I remember fondly. She makes me proud to have grown up in this community.

The black mail carriers had an organization among themselves that promoted family values. They had occasional picnics at the beach house of Mr. Sam Thaggard in Atlantic Beach, South Carolina. Mr. Thaggard's house was right on the beach. At his beach house, we could change clothes, eat, rest, relax, and enjoy each other's company all on this beachfront property.

My mother was a charter member of the local black social club, Jack and Jill of America, which strived to provide culturally enriching experiences for members' children. The Fayetteville Chapter frequently interacted with a similar chapter in Durham, NC. The teen members of Jack and Jill held monthly meetings and potato chip and soft drink social get-togethers several times a year. As Jack and Jillers, we were little socialites, and we would listen to rock and roll music, dance, and eat. It was a high society club, but we managed to enjoy ourselves there.

As a Boy Scout, I enjoyed participating in activities. I rose to the rank of Star Scout before my interest in scouting faded. Scouting focused on character development, and it was a lot of fun. In scouting, we learned first aid, safety procedures and protocols, camping, wholesome family values, and respect for home and country. Being a scout was very fulfilling to me. I acquired leadership skills and so much more during this time of my life.

Another favorite activity was going to the downtown movie theaters: the Colony, Carolina, and Broadway. There was a colored or balcony entrance to all theaters and a white, downstairs entrance for whites. Most of the movies we saw were westerns with cowboys and Indians. Westerns were followed by a weekly serial film and a cartoon. What fun! Admission was nine cents, and popcorn was a dime. We, the black people in the balcony, always cheered for the Indians. Not surprisingly, the cowboys were all white and always defeated the Indians. We cheered for the Indians anyway. Of course, the people sitting below us always cheered for the cowboys.

Occasionally, someone in the balcony would drop a cup of ice or an empty popcorn box off the balcony ledge so that it landed down beneath. The attendant working the balcony would promptly fuss at us when this happened. We denied any knowledge of these incidents, of course.

After the movie ended, we would see it once more, at least to the part where we had started watching it. On the way home, we would stop by the bakery on the opposite end of the street and purchase a pastry treat. At the home bakery, the clerk was so patient with us as we decided how to spend our 15 cents. This was helpful after our theatre incidents. As time passed, we grew more conscious of how the movies depicted people of color. Indians were always losing to the cowboys, and black people were always depicted as illiterate and ignorant, having to be led by whites.

Mama and daddy enjoyed inviting families from church (one at a time) to our house for dinner after Sunday service. Mama would usually prepare ham, roast beef, fried chicken, potato salad, string beans from the garden, tomatoes, and rolls along with iced tea with lemon for our guests. In our family, we each had a favorite piece of chicken. My sister Cynthia loved the wings, I loved the drumsticks, mama preferred the breast, and Daddy did not care for chicken in any form. However, Daddy usually ate the chicken back.

My siblings and I were told by our parents not to eat until the guests were served. One can only imagine our anxiety when a certain visiting priest, ever so slow, would help himself to a wing or drumstick, often two or three. My sister and I would observe his every move while awaiting our turn to fix our plates. We would pray he would hurry up and not eat all of our favorite pieces. We hated for our parents to invite this priest to Sunday dinner. I remember this ever-slow priest more than any other dinner guest.

In the summer, my buddies and I would play football in the large field behind Dr. Vick's office and the Colonial Icehouse on the other side. Sometimes white boys from Hillsboro Street would join us on the field to play football. The games usually ended in a fistfight with name-calling and sometimes bloody noses. Provocative words were often the spark of fights. The whites would call us niggers and we would call them crackers. Then it was on! The next day or so, we would resume our ball playing, forgetting what happened the day before. As you may

imagine, each game ended with a repeat of the previous day's fight. Perhaps our fist fighting, which concluded each baseball game, exposed underlying racial tensions which surfaced during the heat of our games. Our behavior, although wrong, was representative of the deep level of animosity that was growing within the larger community.

Chapter 10: SOME RESIDENTS OF MOORE STREET

The Moore Street residents were like family to each other. We celebrated accomplishments of individual families and attended funerals of our beloved neighbors. There was a strong comradery amongst the community, and everyone looked out for one another. The legacies of our family bloodlines have continued through the years and will live for generations to come. Thinking back on this heritage, I must name and honor these amazing Moore Street families:

Mr. and Mrs. Coppage were both educators and public-spirited individuals. He was an administrator at Fayetteville State Teachers College, and she was a public-school teacher at Lewis Chapel Elementary School.

Mr. and Mrs. Benjamin Ferguson. Mr. Ferguson was a pioneer postal worker who also was a civic leader, long active in the NAACP and other community organizations. His children distinguished themselves in the field of education. Their daughter Inez became the wife of Lt. Colonel Easley and was an administrator in the Fayetteville City School's Central Administrative Office.

Miss Theresa Payne was a quiet educator who taught at local public schools. She was a faithful member of St. Joseph's Episcopal Church and sang in the choir. She would eventually become a benefactor of the church organ guild.

Mr. and Mrs. Jerry Hollingsworth were both educators and business owners. Mr. Hollingsworth operated J's Grill on Hillsboro Street, which was located next to Garris Funeral Home. J's Grill was a popular restaurant and hang-out for young adults. It always enjoyed an outstanding reputation for its clean environment, excellent service, and good food.

Mr. Rob Murchison resided at the corner of Moore and Frink Streets. He maintained a neat home and a well-kept yard. Mr. Rob was known for his love of baseball. He was always seen carrying his transistor radio, which was tuned to a ball game. Mr. Rob was seen daily walking to the corner grocery store, Cashwells Grocery, carrying a six-pack of Coca-Cola empties and returning with a fresh pack of cokes usually around 10:00 AM each morning. His daughter,

Marie became a teacher. His son became a principal of Newbold Training School on campus at Fayetteville State.

Miss Dora. During an era when mainly white men wore starched collared white shirts, Miss Dora was a one-person laundry. She washed and perfectly ironed shirts for commercial purposes. Her backyard always had a large black kettle sitting on a low fire with a light grayish liquid inside. She ironed with irons heated on her wood-fired kitchen stove.

Mr. Kellogg or Kellogg, as everyone called him, always dressed in a clean white tee shirt and white khaki pants. He was the cook at Jones Tourist Home where many people dined after church services. Remember this was an era when people of color were prohibited by law from patronizing white restaurants. However, many people of color would eat Sunday evening meals at Jones Tourist Home, a stately, white house located in the middle of Moore Street. It sat opposite the present-day First Baptist Church. Jones Tourist Home served delicious meals typical of the day: fried chicken, ham, roast beef, rice and gravy, rolls, collard greens, macaroni and cheese, iced tea, and other great dining choices.

Dr. Herbert and Mrs. Jessie Vick. Dr. Vick was a general practice physician who was beloved by the community as well as his wife, Mrs. Jessie Vick. Dr. Vick built his house and medical office on Moore Street, and it was a thriving practice right across the street from our house. The Vicks were among the first people on Moore Street to have a television. Mrs. Vick would invite all the neighborhood children over to watch their favorite tv shows. The shows were in black and white, but the images on the screen offered more than merely listening by radio. It brought us so much pleasure to experience television at the Vick's house.

Dr. C. Mason Quick. Dr. Quick and Mrs. Quick resided across the street from St. Joseph's Episcopal Church in a house formerly occupied by Mrs. Quick's parents, Dr. and Mrs. Melchur. Dr. Quick opened his Eye, Ear, and Nose office at that site.

Dr. James Douglas and Mrs. Mable Douglas. The Douglas family consisted of Dr. and Mrs. Douglas and four children: Sandra, James "Dee Dee," Gail, and Charles. Dr. Douglas was a dentist who had an office on Person Street. Years later his son and grandson both became dentists in Fayetteville.

Mr. and Mrs. Olen Gerald were solid citizens on Moore Street. For many years, their family-owned Hillsboro Taxi, one of the major Black taxi firms in Fayetteville.

Elder and Mrs. Stephens. Elder and Mrs. Stephens were also solid citizens of Moore Street. He was a Presiding Elder for the Methodist Church, and she was a teacher in the public schools. Their sons, Claude and Ralph, grew up to become distinguished professionals in Medicine and Law.

Calvin and Hettie LaHuffman. Mr. and Mrs. LaHuffman were the parents of four children: Margaret, Calvin, Donald, and Cynthia. Our dad was a mail carrier and entrepreneur.

Reverend and Mrs. C.R. Edwards. The Edwards moved to Moore Street when First Baptist Church was built there. Reverend Edwards was a legendary pastor of the church and civic leader in our city.

Mr. Joe's Café. Frink Street ran beside our house at the corner of Moore and Frink Streets. About four houses up the street was a two-story cinderblock building that housed Joe's Store and Café. The owner lived above the Café. Mrs. Hattie was the operator and main worker there. The store featured an assortment of penny candy, soda, pops, cookies, kits, pickled pig feet, potato chips, pickles, bubble gum, and all types of goodies children craved. Ms. Hattie would serve up hearty meals after 6:00 p.m. for construction workers who typically dined on collard greens, rice and gravy, cornbread, pinto beans, stew, ribs, and other hearty foods. All of this was prepared and served by Ms. Hattie, who was a lady of few words, but always pleasant to us kids.

Williams Drug Store was situated at the intersection of Moore and Hillsboro Streets. It was a drug store that sold prescription medicine, comic books, magazines, newspapers, female beauty products. Most importantly to us kids, the store sold ice cream, fountain sodas, milkshakes, candy, and gum. My sister and I as well as others went to the drug store every Sunday after Sunday School to spend some of our weekly allowance of 25 cents. We usually purchased a comic book, candy, and soda. The store was a meeting place for people in the neighborhood to chat.

The above-named residents made Moore Street what it was back then. I will always remember their kindness, comradery, and support. Moore Street today is not the same community that we once inhabited. Nevertheless, our solid foundation was built in this community and from this foundation, the legacies of our fathers and forefathers will live for generations to come. I will always be proud to call the Moore Street community my home. I felt compelled to write this story for a historical perspective and to share the legacy of an exceptional place in the story of Fayetteville, the All-American City.

Epilogue

Today, Moore Street is a far cry from what it was between 1942 and the 1960s. Ironically, this iconic neighborhood, which gave rise to a generation of settled, accomplished black homeowners, is now populated by transient and homeless people. The once neat homes are gone, as well as the playground. Only St. Joseph's Episcopal Church and First Baptist Church remain as symbols of hope and life for the neighborhood. Moore Street represents what a strong community is capable of when its citizens work hard to succeed in life. Fayetteville now has its second black mayor and a predominantly Black City Council, which appears to be focusing on revitalizing neglected parts of the city. If past achievements are precedents for the future, Moore Street may rise once again from the ashes

of dispossession and vacancy to a glistening
dawn symbolizing the power of a community to
flourish even in the midst of darkness.

About the Author

onald W. LaHuffman is a 1960 graduate from E.E. Smith High in Fayetteville, North Carolina. Subsequently, he attended North Carolina College at Durham, now North Carolina Central University, earning a Bachelor of Arts in Psychology in 1964. Later he obtained a Master of Arts degree in Education in 1969. He completed the Education for Ministry Program from the University of the South. His career spanned decades as a high school teacher and administrator at the college and state levels.

He and his devoted wife of over 55 years, Jean Hodges LaHuffman, have three adult children. Donna, Joey, and Renee are all college graduates and professionals. They have a total of four grandchildren and three of them are also college graduates and professionals. The

youngest grandchild is still in high school, and
two great-grandsons are the newest additions to
this accomplished family. Finally, the author is
a lifelong member of St. Joseph's Episcopal
Church where he is recognized as Senior
Warden, Emeritus.